Last Stanza
Poetry Journal

Issue #9: Synesthesia
Edited by Jenny Kalahar
Linda Wesolowski, artist

Stacktreed
Press

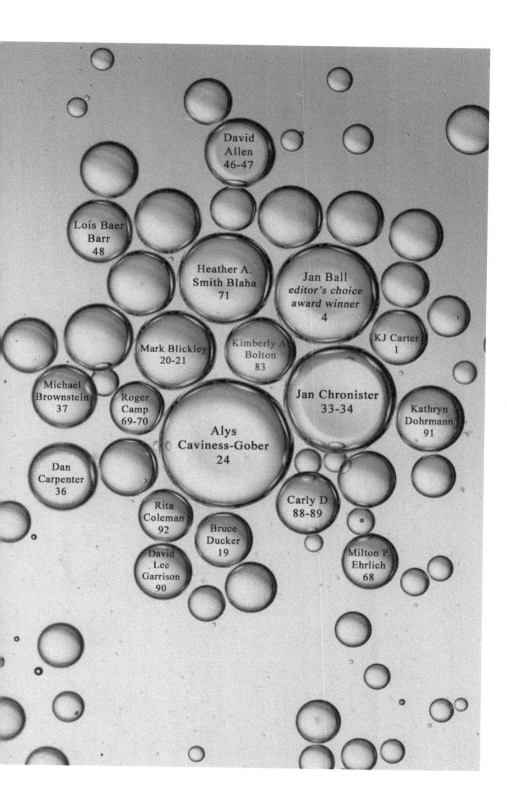

David
Allen
46-47

Lois Baer
Barr
48

Heather A.
Smith Blaha
71

Jan Ball
*editor's choice
award winner*
4

Mark Blickley
20-21

Kimberly A.
Bolton
83

KJ Carter
1

Michael
Brownstein
37

Roger
Camp
69-70

Jan Chronister
33-34

Kathryn
Dohrmann
91

Alys
Caviness-Gober
24

Dan
Carpenter
36

Rita
Coleman
92

Bruce
Ducker
19

Carly D
88-89

David
Lee
Garrison
90

Milton P.
Ehrlich
68

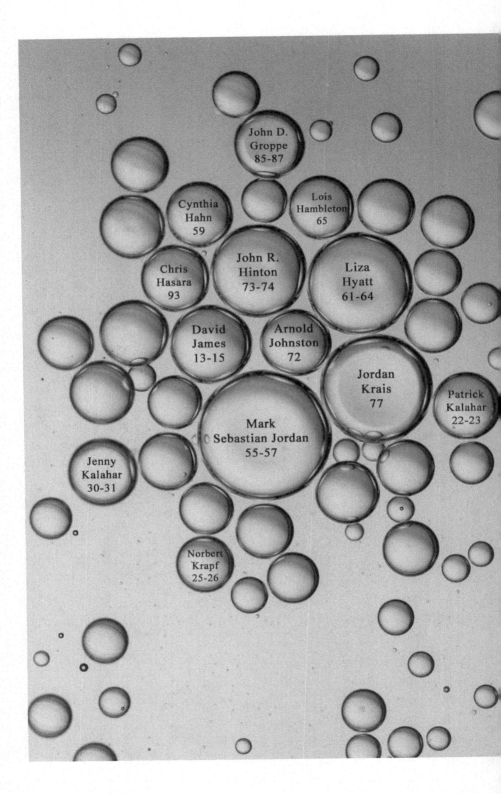

John D.
Groppe
85-87

Cynthia
Hahn
59

Lois
Hambleton
65

Chris
Hasara
93

John R.
Hinton
73-74

Liza
Hyatt
61-64

David
James
13-15

Arnold
Johnston
72

Jordan
Krais
77

Patrick
Kalahar
22-23

Mark
Sebastian Jordan
55-57

Jenny
Kalahar
30-31

Norbert
Krapf
25-26

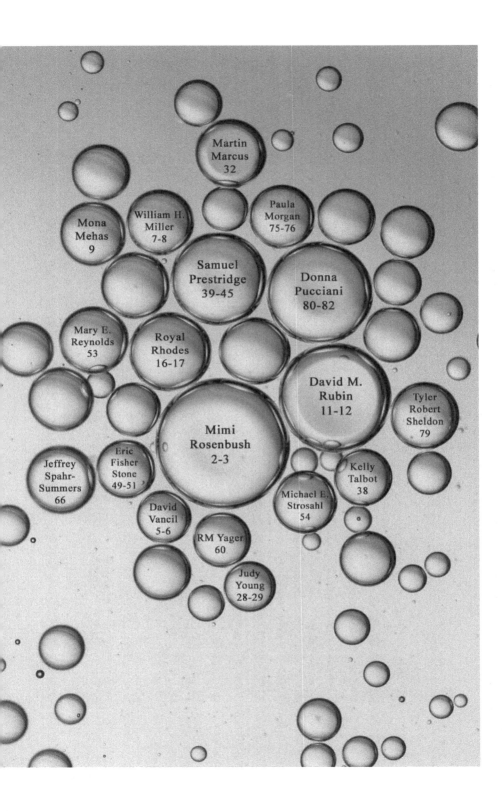

Martin
Marcus
32

Mona
Mehas
9

William H.
Miller
7-8

Paula
Morgan
75-76

Samuel
Prestridge
39-45

Donna
Pucciani
80-82

Mary E.
Reynolds
53

Royal
Rhodes
16-17

David M.
Rubin
11-12

Tyler
Robert
Sheldon
79

Jeffrey
Spahr-
Summers
66

Eric
Fisher
Stone
49-51

Mimi
Rosenbush
2-3

Kelly
Talbot
38

David
Vancil
5-6

Michael E.
Strosahl
54

RM Yager
60

Judy
Young
28-29

The Return

Smoke from the shelling drifted with the wind,
   ashes blocking rays of the sun.
Just last month, I walked this path with my neighbors
   as we celebrated our blessings,
      our mayor leading us with spirit like a marching band.

Today, he leads us back to our village
like the phantom drum major of a macabre band
   of shattered souls,
my eyes drawn to debris covering
   what was left of our street,
watching for any hint of what had been,
praying in the dark gray haze
   for any sign of life in the damage—
      a violin broken, resting on a smashed chair,
      a pram upside down, empty now.
Sitting in the swing that once held my children,
   my eyes are drawn to a small patch of grass.
   Nestled in the blades are my spring flowers.
   Life, despite all the destruction: life.
It was then that I could finally weep, releasing pain.

KJ Carter

The Color Two in April

When I begin a long drive at four in the morning,
the dark is without color but for a splash
of egg-yellow headlights on my windshield.

It doesn't register that yellow means three
because it's too early for that kind of thinking,
and finding I-55 south of Chicago is all that matters.

In spite of the four am, the idea of number four
alludes me. I'm too excited to be on the road,
so four—a shouting blaze of orange and red—is subverted.

A podcast keeps me company. Two people are talking
as if I'm in the same room, but they don't stop
for the color two appearing around us. Around me.

I've never actually experienced the number two,
but I recognize it right away.

It has a sound silent to the touch,
so I turn off the podcast in reverence.

I have known this color since I was young,
when numbers and letters began their chromatic life.

Brushing the barren land with its tender blue-grey veil,
the color two touches my hands through the steering wheel.

I drive wrapped in sweet feathers of twos,
while at the same time aware of the road ahead.

The day breaks through in threes and fours,
but the touch of two lingers like a longing.

Mimi Rosenbush

The Riddle of the Color Three

like birds
in trees,
not wall nor chair,

the three
survives
outside in air

with hue of sun
yet with-
out light

nothing to do
with brightness
or sight

blinding yellow,
I yield
to its hope

full of dreams,
awakened,
awoke

Mimi Rosenbush

Passion Fruit Youth

We gave them our passion fruit youth,
the peaches of our honey intensity,
and we loved them as they licked
us clean as a mango stone
before we gradually dried up
like sweet apricots and switched
from subtle earth-tone clinging dresses
to watermelon-pink elastic-waist cargo pants
and matching pastel T-shirts.

Now, unable to maneuver alone
along the soft Florida beach
with our canes or walkers,
our husbands guide us to deck chairs
at the water's edge where the sand is harder,
gripping our arms like raspberry children
who need assistance.

I am mesmerized by the silver alewives
all facing one direction beyond the sandbars,
glittering sequins on the tips of waves,
before factory ships arrive to crunch them
into a strawberry smoothie.

Jan Ball
Editor's choice award winner

Elegy for Ellis Marsalis, Jr., Jazz Musician and Teacher

November 14, 1934 – April 1, 2020

Ellis, once you proclaimed, "Never disrespect Al Hirt,"
not only because he broke the color line and put you
in his band, but because he could play. "I heard you
when the band stopped at my college to share jazz
on your way to New Orleans, and I liked 'Cotton Candy,'"
I bragged. "But they stuck you where they hold rodeos."

You scoffed, "We played in all kinds of places," lowering
your eyelids as you smiled, so I'd know it was the playing
that mattered, never the trappings. I wish I'd told you
I never forgot how your hands moved like cool liquid over
ivory keys as your head bobbed and you kept the time.

I imagine a song thrush alighting on a slack black wire
stretched from a pole standing close to your cozy home
proclaiming its insistent melody. Beside a window opened
to let in the April breeze, I see one of your six sons cock
his head and hear him say, "That is our father singing."

The piano fallboard's been shut, the bass
packed in its case, and the sax put aside,
yet we stop to take stock and to listen.

David Vancil

Chameleon in the Kitchen

Sunlight coats the marble-white linoleum floor
with long, thick swatches stretching luridly
through a lens fashioned by tall, clear glass.

I slide the door open just a smidgeon to let in
the dog. A sly lizard slips in beneath a paw
like a sneak thief, transforming its color from
emerald to ethereal ash like the clinging tip
of a smoked cigarette. Amid the din of my dog's
yapping, I gape open-mouthed as the chameleon
squeezes deftly under the hulking, white stove.

A lifeless statue, I sit in a kitchen chair
restraining my moiling mutt by its collar, breathing
in shallow gasps that rattle in my chest.

I've left the sliding door cracked open to enable
the chameleon's great escape, waiting to witness
light transforming itself like waves of sound.

I am only barely more patient than the hound.

David Vancil

Between Sand and Sea

after Rachel Carson

I look to see what's happening
on this strip between sand and sea,
watching creatures build hopeless homes,
careless ripples massaging my toes,
and a gold-speckled beetle glide
between unwearying waves.

I wonder if these breakers will bring
salt-stained treasure or rotting timber
from a wreck? Can a touch of sea
unify us all? I find a moment where
nothing happens, when the waves
at their leisure end the flow of time
with a final shoreward surge.

I leave the beach thinking
that the beetle and I
are as unsteady as the sea.
Take care, little one, as you
skim the waves,
teeth nipping
at your belly—
you know you can't swim.

William H. Miller

Lazarus, Who Never Comes

You can find her where
the graveled road ebbs,
turning to clay at the river's
bank. Under a canopy
of fir and alder, you push
through high grass.
There rests her remaining,
her immensity of girth.
Splintered spoil
leans hard on dogwood branches;
crushed seedlings call
for Lazarus, who never comes.
A home for squirrels,
seasonal flocks,
head-sized honeycombs,
greedy grubworms
in the wound
where the untamed tempest
disemboweled her.
Weak in timber, strong
in saplings, she did not need
a timepiece. If she could yearn,
she would be the ginkgo
surviving Hiroshima,
a middle-aged Methuselah.

Morning—
darkness comes anew,
leaden rumbles, electricity
sweeping up the valley.
She hears with tired arms
and ruined strength.
We watch—and wait—

William H. Miller

Home

Home in the air, in their ears.

He dances in the flowers,
pink perfume electrifying,
crawls on his belly
absorbing purple sweetness,
undulates yellow
and swings dizzy,
covered in pollen.
Orange blended to intoxicate.

She wakes in shimmering golden leaves.
They sparkle russet,
falling on her from the
deep-green canopy,
shades of brown anticipation
meditating within her.
Red for strength.

Rapture when they come together,
kaleidoscope leaves and
bountiful flowers swinging—
whispers in the ether
of home.

Mona Mehas

Traumerie

Irreversible inhibition. Enzymes transforming vitamins.
Words from fog. *Back to useful states.*
An army of attendants. Doctors. Nurses. Alienists.
One cannot discern their intentions.
If my heart beat any faster, it would hurl itself
across the tiles and out to the world.
The young man visits each day
when the sun has passed.
An angel from a future without me. Florestan. Eusebio. Hermes.
Mercury.
Prevent damage from oxidation.
They feed me poison which makes me unable to talk,
then seem angry that I don't try. Without a name,
my story is not accessible. A name is key.
Hermes is a name. Mercurial flits about.
They say many times *nerves flitting about.*
Many quills and papers are pushed at me, towards me.
Are they meaning for me to reveal a secret? How would I even hold a quill,
an object?
The young angel pushes my chair to the fortepiano and
makes a show of expecting me to play.
My hand throbs,
but my other can't reach to squeeze it.
The black keys are repugnant metal,
placed to weaken me further. I hear a noise like muffled yelling
coming from deep inside me.
The angel plays effortlessly
with a reach that is beyond personal. He is me
or has become me.
He plays songs whose names I know. *Kreisleriana, Carnaval.*
Dichterliebe, Dichterliebe remains.
I will remain a model of dignity
confronted by these strange angels and what has been stolen.

He plays a new song and says "Brahms."
Brahms.

He says he has been sent by family.
I must have been blessed with family.
Once upon a time, my life existed
out there and was taken from me.
Precious wife and partner. Brilliant children.
Words from a shopping list or an obituary.
Many children, and some are dead. A name is one's key,
one's infinite series of chords.
All is melody. *Traumerie.*
I have no key, no past, and no song.
With great fanfare, they usher a woman
dressed in black to my threshold. Frail and defiant,
she is the symbol of all humanity,
lost but more powerful than an angel.
An angel in mourning for me.
Stale mourning, as if she'd experienced my parting long ago.
They hold her elbows, but she refuses to faint and would hold
and kiss my face if they released her to venture closer.
They say a word, but I can't make it out.
Her key is Clarity.
She smiles and points, "Schumann." The pain sears
as if a crown of thorns squeezes tight around my temples
and presses light from my eyes.
Water putting out a candle.
A cleansing, a baptism.
Ice cold water to wash away everything like the flood
fills my nose and lungs and mouth and insides.
Washes over this broken foreign body.

David M. Rubin

Big Love

I ended up dissecting love again
after living forty-three years married to the same woman.

On a table wiped clean with alcohol,
I cut our love open down the middle,
spread it apart, to find this:
                              a thimbleful of red tears,
                                  a whoopee cushion,
                               two four-leaf clovers,
              a palmful of forgiveness that looked like granola,
                              several Ahmad tea bags,
                  recipes for biscotti and cracker-toffee,
                   dozens of unused theatre tickets,
                         a blow-up water lounge,
                                  two golf balls.

It smelled like patience,
like understanding,
and after I sewed it shut,
the stitches dissolved completely
as it healed itself.

Every year, I dissect love
trying to determine
how it works, how it stays and grows,
and each year
my list is different.

Last year, I found yarn,
notebooks, eggnog, a bear hug, a kilt,
mango hard cider, darts, corned beef and cabbage.
The year before, there were Christmas ornaments,
fuchsia petals, several fat quarters, a book of poems,
baby clothes, a half-cup of marvel
with some wonder sprinkled on top.

Each dissection
is unpredictable, and each one surprises me,
but I've decided to stop.
I haven't figured out
a damn thing about love
other than
there's no map or secret to it,
no magic trick or potion.

It's snow falling, a bluebird in the maple,
the perfect gin and tonic, the smell of your hair,
an almost-full moon in the cloudless sky,
a dog barking across the golf course,
the chimes ringing at the bottom
of the stairs as I wake up
to find you
lying
beside
me.

David James

A Matter of Time

"I was lugging my death from Kampala to Krakow."
— C.K. Williams, "The Coffin Store"

Every morning when I set my feet on the ground,
death wakes and climbs on my back.

I can't feel him or her, but the older I get,
the more I know I'm lugging around

that final gasp baked into my DNA.
On a park bench, in a cute little vacation shack

on the big lake, in a hotel room along I-69,
my day will arrive.

I'll bargain and pray, hoping against hope for some slack
in the rules, but fail. Like everyone.

So savor the tortellini and the smell of the rind
as you peel a sweet mandarin. Revel in your son's laugh,

the new mums on the porch, two jays fighting at the bird feeder.
When the first leaves turn red, I don't think of it as a dire sign.

I smile like a baby and look everywhere with my eyes of clay.

David James

The Ferryman

I remember some things—
the crossroads, the empty,
earthy space, and leaves
floating in slow departure.

He was waiting at a crossing
place on the shoreline,
had always been there,
beached in the quiet shallows.

His gaunt fingers knuckled
on the handles, the steady
rhythm of oars
marking commas in the water,

licking the ancient boards.
The weight I added to the boat
carrying all pain and delight;
a penny sours my tongue.

The starless sense of time loosens,
receding from who I once was
as boat and oars furrow the surface
like a last, lingering caress.

A shanty town or death camp
shimmers on the horizon line,
smudged as if by thick woodsmoke
from the blackened tree line.

Morning coughs into wakefulness,
and little lamps in the gloom
expand from shadow to gold,
igniting this instant fire.

No one loves, I know.
No one remains to love.
Yet there is only loving left,
slipping through our fingers.

Royal Rhodes

Space

The silence that comes after
a clap of thunder
instructs, circumscribes
a silence we'd otherwise miss.
Did Henry Moore think
we would prefer his woman
to the donut hole?
Space comes easily to painters
who decide what to leave out,
to sculptors who reveal the idea
by discarding superfluous stone.
When Bach removes the third,
our ear puts it back. And so,
we seat ourselves in the fifth section
of the orchestra reserved for
composers.

Bruce Ducker

Mysterious Waters of the Naked and Nervous

She begins her life
along with nine thousand seven hundred and fourteen siblings
in the shallowest part of the pond
just four days after being laid as a jelly egg
attached to a fern leaf bent over humid water.

On day seven, she sallies to neighboring weeds
using a very circular route,
quietly clings to a weed, watches with terror
as brothers and sisters are attacked
by sharp-beaked birds of varying hues
swooping to chew helpless tadpoles,
devouring membranes covering their gills and necks.

One of few tadpoles to survive to day ten,
she officially becomes a tiny pitch-black pollywog
with continuously wiggling tail and small round mouth
of horny jaws that scrape across tiny plants,
searching for something to eat.

She greedily swallows microscopic animals
found inside pond-bottom ooze
and slime clinging to the pond's surface.

Feasting on a particularly tasty ooze meal,
she is horrified to witness
tadpole brothers and sisters eating each other,
siblings extending their bellies
by swallowing extended family.

Mostly tail with a fine stippling of gold,
within twenty-four hours, she breathes
from two gills at each side of her throat
as hind legs suddenly sprout
rounded buds that soon turn into toes,

amazed at how fast she can propel
away from murderous dive-bombing birds of color.

She first demonstrates courage
by a successful attack of black fish that menace her for hours,
sucking on its fish fins until they are ragged,
not in anger or self-defense,
more for tasty algae trapped within them.

But it does feel good to be able to destroy instead of being destroyed.

Mark Blickley

Listening to Xenakis, Penderecki, and Gubaidulina

Music that foreshadows a future dream:
a house on fire, burning memories;
shadows you can smell in a dark alley;
a broken doll's head with brains exposed,
wet with imagined clarity;
the texture of a single trumpet's magenta scream;
multitudes awaiting the annihilation.

A wind unseen, known only by its aftermaths,
trundles across a flat, arid land.
Dead leaves caught in fallen branches
shake like unfurling sails,
and stalks of prairie grass,
browned by despair,
bend downward in obeisance
to an unwonted *force majeure.*

New voices deny the void
and vibrate with crystalline hues.
Tendrilling ganglia reach and stretch
to create new synapses,
only to be blocked.
Lacking the vision,
we cannot see the sounds.

Patrick Kalahar

The Obscurantism of Light

Does light obscure the shadows?
Is reality as tenuous
as an ephemerid's footprints
upon the pond?
Is sadness found in the silences
between the rasping of the frogs?
Is the bending and rumbling trembling
of the shore grass
a token of surrender to the wind?

Is meaning measured out with eyedroppers
as an antidote to despair,
and will I try to find a new path
through the muck and mud
in this intermediate place
or return the way I came
along firmer ground?

Patrick Kalahar

Four

is a number flowing purple
like a floral-paisley tartan
in a lilac-scented dream

The Sound of You

firecrackers echoing
around corners and over rooftops
and mysterious rustling alleyways
and liquid jazz murmuring across
a silent, darkened lake
and sticky hot caresses of
a summer breeze muffling
against the back of my neck
and of course
a tango

Alys Caviness-Gober

What This Poem Wants

I want you to inhale and ingest me,
become part of your bloodstream.
I want to go down into your psyche
and enter into your spirit. Want you
to see with me, breathe with me.
Also want to walk with you,
help you find your rhythm,
go on a journey with you.
Want to give you energy,
vision, purpose. Want to give
you power, a sense that you
can make things happen
for yourself and for others.
Want you to realize that
you can heal yourself and help
the world heal. Want you to
discover you can grow
even after your body reaches
its full size so that the cells
of your creativity keep dividing
and your spirit becomes larger
and larger. See, your vision
has already increased. You feel
you are part of a larger whole
and respect and value all the parts
of the universe in which you
are glad to live. You feel a song
about to come out of your mouth.
Clay wants to become bowl
when you touch and shape it
with your fingertips. Paper wants
to host your pencil drawings
of plants, animals, and people.
Words want to become stories
when you breathe them awake.

Stories want to slip into poems
when you tell them in such
a way that people feel their
rhythms and start to move
and shake in what we can
only call a dance of the folk.
Now I have come fully alive
inside you. I have found a home.
You have given me new life.
You will pass me on to others
who will breathe and feel
my rhythms and movements
as they make them their own
rhythm and dance and create
a vision that others can see,
shape, expand, and share.

                    Norbert Krapf

Spring Storm

Dark clouds
piling and rolling
like kittens
in a basket

Rain pouring down,
silver sheets
falling into a pewter river
streaked with sterling,
twisting through woods'
shadowed ebony

Judy Young

Twilight

Under the yews and oak
where the shadows never leave,
rows of opal-pale headstones
crookedly line the ancient graves.
Dim shade evokes solitude,
mournful doves cry rueful laments,
wings rustling amid the leafy branches,
raucous inky crows call
goodnight to no one in particular.
Dark clouds hide the sunset as
lightning flickers at sky's rim
promising an unquiet twilight
at woods' end.

Judy Young

This Root a Pulse

Firm pulsebeats shock the nerves
of my palm and fingers.
This raw root I hold is alive,
its surrounding black clods of soil like extraneous flesh,
clinging to brown, fragile tendril veins.

I cannot see movement,
but feel within silence a call for spring.
And then I hear it:
a violin-like solo
played on thin, untangling contractile roots,
nearly imperceptible,
hushed as peat bog:
a song for rain,
for solid ground to settle in.

I hum along as I bury what may be amaryllis
or yellow queen hyacinth,
pour water just so,
wetting to enliven
and then stand aside,
dirty hands planted on satisfied hips.
And still I hum,
calling for warm rain to gulp,
a patch of earth to live within,
and roots of my own.

Jenny Kalahar

Ami

Buttercups remember favorite bees—
the feel of sturdy legs against petals,
the sight of specific patterns of pollen-dotted black.
Dreaming of them in golden moonlight,
the flowers ache for sunlight to stream across the swaying meadow,
bringing with it morning sounds and an old, familiar buzz.

Maize

In cornfields no longer planted in rows,
headless stalks hold green hands in shared grief.
Though still warmed by the long summer afternoon,
they're chilled by the loss of children.
When I enter this cornfield,
the feather-wind from seed-seeking birds
seems far heavier than words can say.

Jenny Kalahar

Canvas

I can paint a poem,
hold it up at the end of my arm,
turn it left, right
to find just the light.

I don't mean some protracted narrative or epic—
you can't see them on your easel.
They live buried to the neck in pages,
long, thready things on spools
no two eyes can take in at once.

My poem is born and sickens
on the single sheet.
I touch it here with crimson,
there I overpaint it (for a thicker sense).
I come back from the other room
to find it needs paling.

I ball it up, release it,
and see where the wrinkles lie.

                          Martin Marcus

Lake Superior Blue

If I took a photo
to the paint store,
matched the lake with
one of their chips,
what would the name
turn out to be?

Something frivolous
like *Navy Satin, Fresh Hyacinth,
Crisp French Blue?*
Some sparkling shade
like *Bright Sailing,
Periwinkle,* or *Sapphire?*

Chemicals can't
replicate a body of water
that breathes snow,
creates icy hues
on the horizon.

There is no other way
to describe what is simply
Lake Superior Blue.

Jan Chronister

Shady Nook School, 1955

Our blocks were sawed-up
2x4s, their edges sanded smooth.
We colored worksheets printed
on ditto machines,
inhaled the aroma
of sweet purple ink.

During kindergarten playtime,
Danny Hines threw a block
at another boy.
Blood ran down
his forehead,
dripped on teacher's fluffy white rug.

We steered clear of Danny at recess,
played hide-and-seek behind huge trees,
hung from monkey bars,
carried the sharp scent of metal
back inside on our palms.

Did Danny go to Vietnam?
End up in prison? A boardroom?
All I know for sure
is blood dried darkly
on that rug.

Jan Chronister

Dreaming the Doctor

After Sophie Laffitte's biography

My heart smells a rich brown hue
like lumps of Volga and Yenisei
Chekhov stirred into his morning tea
whose scarlet stench already
heralded the lethal hemorrhage
behind the chronic cough.

I savor with him the caress of birdsong,
the sharp taste of leaden Steppes wind,
soon to give way to clamor of paper—
schools and libraries to build and furnish
as well as the massive immortal *oeuvre*—
jolting him back to work.

At his front door, patients line up
bearing their miseries like tributes.
The great man hears these pages I turn,
rattling toward his early death
while they forge a hymn that bears me,
awed to shame, unaccountably upward.

Dan Carpenter

Early Spring Storm
A Waltmarie

within the context of hush, a vocabulary of whispers
snow fell
time was not essential—Friday evening into Saturday morning
quiet
the valley filled itself with white evergreens
no wind
an infinity of snowflakes erased sight lines, landscapes
silver
we went into the fields tobogganing snow angels
ice warm.

Michael Brownstein

The Flow

My body is water.
The fist passes through me,
and I remain unchanged.
The fist, too, is water.
The space between us
is water. There is no space.
There is no between.
We are all one ocean,
and the flows are but motion.
Drops do not exist.
We all melt into each other.

The other man believes
he is attacking me.
But he is not other.
He is me. I am him.
Water pours through water.
It is as if a part of myself
is temporarily unaware
that we are one.
We are a crosscurrent,
surging through ourself.

I am everything.
Everything is nothing.
I dissolve
until all is water.

Kelly Talbot

After Decades of Work as a Corpse

Outside Grauman's, he tripped and fell face-first
into wet concrete, stayed there five hours.
When the crowd thinned some, attendant workers
jack-hammered him free. He walked to his hearse,
got in, and drove off.
No one thought too much about it: after
his *corpse run over by a Bush Hog*; after
corpse imploding in a spaceship speeding
toward a black hole, folk were harder to please.
They wanted splashier catastrophes.

He wakes at 5:00 a.m., still, calls his ex
to feel dead enough inside, and rises to start
his daily grind. Black coffee and burnt toast
with tar-pit marmalade. He hits the gym:
core work, free weights, treadmill to keep his weight
cadaverous. Afterward, a shower.
Nine a.m., he's scheduling the day's shots:
corpse of self-immolated Buddhist monk
mauled by feral dogs; mime as corpse tartare
in a zombie buffet. The requisite
decapitations. He's pioneered four
different categories, myriad
subsections.
        It's his craft: green screens, latex
maulery, chroma-key software, braces
for rigor mortis, his brilliant, grotesque
prosthetics, mindfulness meditation
to sustain his multi-million-dollar
death grimace.
        Each scene pays ten thousand bucks:
corpse shot 14 times through a car windshield;
corpse of skydiver with necrotizing
fasciitis whose spare chute failed and who
was fished out of an active volcano.
He checks his database, tweaks, and invents.

Make-up, minutes posing, no editing—
by definition—uploading the shot.
He stays busy and doesn't read the trades.
He doesn't need scripts, answers inquiries
with *How did I die?* He shoots some fifty,
sixty scenes a week.
                              He's only done one
promotional tour. Dragged on stage and heaped
in the spotlight, he refused to answer
questions, humiliating the emcee.
You'd call him lucky at the start—chosen
from a cattle call, he made the casting
director *believe* he was dead even
as he read the scene, contorted thusly.
After that first role, there were dues to pay:
screen guild wages, chump bit parts--*stumped remains
of gator frenzy, rotted Nazi ten.*
Then, his big break—on the autopsy slab
five hours straight, he remained in character
when the dimmest son of the prop master
thought he was a mannequin. Dragging him
to the warehouse, the boy stopped for a smoke,
struck a match on his face. Powers that be
notice things like that. Focus groups *believed*
he was dead. Protestors castigated
studios for mutilating corpses.
The suits were smart enough to keep quiet—
a plausible deniability.
He issued no disclaimer and kept low,
developing his database, working
at his art: *sunbaked corpse in a life raft,
gull savaged;* various asphyxias
(auto-erotic, carbon monoxide);
*corpse of crash survivor eaten alive
by ex-girlfriend.*

Offers rained down on him
when focus groups found the same film better
with him than without, bumped the bottom line
(deride the profit motive as you will)
the breadth of a death rattle. His seconds
on screen (*corpse of a Black Friday shopper;*
radiation victim found rat-ravaged
in a dumpster) left the toughest critic
gasping for breath.
             He could have marketed
bottled water or an exercise craze.
If someone wrote the *Mr. Death Diet,*
it would make *The New York Times Book Review*
He gave it all up for death, perfection
of his gruesome craft: *drowning victim sucked*
through industrial desalinator;
corpse digested, disgorged by Great White shark
and peeled from UV overexposure.
This last, a public service announcement:

"Nine out of ten dermatologists say:
'Sunblock ... use it! Whatever else happens,
no one wants to leave a leathery stiff.'"

He keeps a low profile, avoiding fans,
inventing deaths not thought about for films
not yet proposed.
             If he goes out, he walks,
hat pulled low. He gave up on autographs
years ago, but wannabes surround him.
Some drop to the sidewalk when they see him
gliding along. They give him their headshots.
They give him contortions—*corpse of a man*
under a piano dropped five stories,
man run over by clown-driven trolley.

Some call him out, dumb plebian mimics
of his salad days—tributes not clever,
though one dismemberment he had to stop
and think about. They give him resumes.
He takes them, does nothing, seeing nothing
he has to offer. These days, he's seldom
seen in public. Some say he phones in roles,
but he's never been in greater demand.
Perky young actresses, sylphs with rocket
trajectories, have turned down starring roles
when his is not the suppurating corpse
found beneath the stairs, tucked in nuptial beds,
stowed in the trunk of stepdad's Caddy.
His contortions impossible; his face
always a rictus of off-screen horror.

Samuel Prestridge

Logophobia

Inside the bag, tongues babble, testing
the ruckused sky for gods. *Horse hoof. King snake.*
Red-tailed hawk. A tall, worn man tosses
the burlap sack into the truck bed, takes
another, walks to the shade tree where two men wait.

The word for which they search is not
Agkistrodon contortrix.
                    They'd call it
chunk head, death adder, white oak snake, Southern
copperhead, highland *or* dry-land moccasin,
poplar leaf, red oak, red snake. Whatever
the word, they know chapter and verse where it's found.
In summer, on limestone shelves heated by sunlight
or, in winter, crevasses—loved also
by timber rattlers. Sometimes in fall
on land swapped with the river or in leaf-bed,
they'll find it sunning, minding its own, awaiting
idiot mice.
                    Whatever word they trust,
they still walk lightly, delicately
roust the next rock, test the next crevasse
for heftier words. End of day,
snake-rich and sweaty, they sing about the word
made flesh and undwelling among them.

Lord Jesus, let nothing unholy remain,
Apply Thine own blood and extract every stain;
To get this blest cleansing, I all things forego—
Now wash me, and I shall be whiter than snow.

One cries out words in an undulant, unknown
tongue, words none of them can spell, begins
a dance on the packed, rocky soil. The others
join, lifting hands, as on Sundays when the word
they've gathered is spread on the floor, alive
and curving through stamping feet, taken up,
twining arms, necks, as the minister yells

... Getting back to the Sons of God.
People say they're saved and sanctified.
I'll tell you how much you're sanctified.
As much of his word as you do, that's how much you're sanctified.
The word will abide forever.
You'll die on this earth, but that right there is going to abide forever.

The word abides as homesteads, razed, graded, paved,
become interchanges, off-ramps smelling
of deep fat and diesel. The word abides
as jobs they know to work leave for Bangladesh,
Sumatra, words they couldn't find on a map,
given a fat bag of chance and another
set of hands. The word abides as children
leave for Nashville, buy cowboy hats to wait on
people wearing cowboy hats. The word abides
because, alive in their hands, at their feet,
they take it up, some kissing the wedged,
metallic heads, some clasping them to breast.
A frowsy widow lifts aloft a copperhead,
fat, drowsy, as the dimmest of her sisters
lifts a rat-slack rattler, spins it around
like a nephew. A prom-shirted deacon
screams at both, leans into his screaming ...

There'll be no more sufferin'-uh,
there'll be no more sweat to wipe from the brow-uh,
when we cross over the river Jordan-uh and we go home, and-uh ...

a three-piece band plays a rockabilly
drone, Chuck Berry fed through a chain saw,
and all are dancing, twirling, stamping,
weeping, lifting up whatever word
they use as if God were floating over the church
watching them, listening through the ceiling.

Samuel Prestridge

Fishing for Answers

There's a man I always see
standing at the end of the pier
when I take my lunch walk.
He holds a long pole
and occasionally casts
a line into the bay.
There's no bait on the hook.
The creel at his feet is empty—
almost as empty as the look on his face,
his eyes fixed on the horizon.

One day I asked him what
he hoped to catch.
Without a glance at me,
he pulled his line from the water
and cast it back with a slight groan.
"I'm fishing for answers," he said.
"I tried books, schools, the streets,
and even turned to poetry.
Nothing."

I felt terrible for interrupting his search,
but I had one more question.
"Answers to what?" I asked.
"Everything ... nothing," he said.
I walked on as he recast his line.
His search tormented me.
Was there really something there
in the cold, blue waters of life?
The answer to everything
and nothing?

The answer hit me
like a slap to the face.
The search is the answer.
I bought a fishing rod yesterday.
There's plenty of room on the pier.

David Allen

Synesthetic Potpourri

My husband used to date a girl named Synesthesia.
Synesthesia is not as tasty as spanakopita.
A side effect of Covid19, synesthesia is not long lasting.
The latest bridal bouquets combine baby's breath and synesthesia.
Chartreuse synesthesia mixed with absinthe is the drink of poets.
Kim Addonizio dispelled our synesthesia at her workshop.
Synesthesia is one percent expiration and ninety-nine perspiration.
Don't hide your light under Old Spice deodorant.
WSRS offers soft rock synesthesia for lovers.

Lois Baer Barr

Becoming the Song

Hearing is widely thought to be the last sense to go in the dying process.
—Erik Rolfsen

Senses blending, I hear smells
and light thumping darkness
like immense sails catching wind.

Outside the hospice window, chickadees
rattle alarms for hawks. Higher,
a plane chimes the sky's cirrus-marbled bell.
Ghosts of barn owls whisk from shingles,
blueness thinning to black until
Earth grinds her orbit.

Aluminum slabs of space litter
fizz white noise across the moon. Saturn's rings
groove like records as I fly
to stars singing their chorus.
The swan-bright Milky Way swirls
curdles of static.

Galaxies bejewel the deep,
some spiraled, others spuming eggs
or bridal veils of vapor,
superclusters in spiderwebs
laced together, gossamer strings
strummed by a nameless bow.

Receded light whispers dust,
and silence funnels down my ears.
Someone says goodnight
and goodnight.

Eric Fisher Stone

The Big Dipper

... we came forth, and once more saw the stars.
—Dante's *Inferno*, Robert Pinsky trans.

After six hundred thousand Covid dead
in the states, I drive to a country pasture
so night frogs might cure my grief.

Fireflies glint warm shards over switchgrass
strummed by wind. No freight train bawls
in the dark for what has been or could be.

People aren't harvest mice thrashing for seeds.
We demand gifts from the universe
this azure planet can't provide. Above,

the big dipper buoys seven urchins
in the oceanic dome of space.
Only Earth houses heaven and hell.

In five billion years, the sun
boils all whales of the sea to ash.
Could a mouse tolerate such terms?

I vow skyward in silent vespers
to love Earth like a bride
so the stars may remember the world.

                                    Eric Fisher Stone

Philosophy is Preparation for Death

Socrates said in the *Phaedo*. I'll die
in battle like a Viking, except I'd fight

the fear of death, my brain wrestling
my skull's crumbling theatre.

I'd hold a teddy bear, not a sword;
my Valhalla, the loam's birthday cake.

The more I love the world, the less
I believe in heaven, nothing

richer than lizards or winged thimbles
of beetles. I'll die dancing, my jazzy knees

clanging, an old toddler
spinning in a yellow meadow,

calling kindness between all moles
celled among grubs, snakes, or Falstaff

who babbled of green fields.
My death becomes a second birth,

to face my ashes playing with dinosaurs
and sandboxes. One day, the void summons

me from my bread-hot deathbed
when snowfall cankers cow pastures,

my breath empties, and childhood
boils between my ears, lost

to infinite black space. My blood
belongs to Earth. I'll die in love with love.

Eric Fisher Stone

Introduction and Allegro

Reminiscent of November sky, an aura of fog
hung above everything that Sunday afternoon in May.
Driving from city to suburbs the long way,
I tuned the radio to WFMT.

Music of Maurice Revel flowed
over budding branches, intricate filigree lacework.
Lawns suddenly resurrected to accompany
harp arpeggio, ethereal flute ensemble.

At a red light, tulips hid their colors
enclosed by the green bract, saying,
it's too cold today. Magnolias showed
precocious bloom, and I saw the music of spring.

Harp and flute filled the air with expectation:
prelude to life eternal. Isn't allegro
the tempo of our life—often joyous but short?

The light turned green. Go on. Be moved.
Go with the light of your epiphany
full of haze, music, daydreams, and drive.

Mary E. Reynolds

Symphony on McKinley's Hill

Monday's violin
walks a conversation
up the stairs,
down the asphalt
with a cello's struggle
about to give up.

Saturday stories and the
sins of Sunday,
heavy hymnal breaths,
hands held through the pews,
first love and confessions—
stolen kisses and Hail Mary
with her long golden hair,
blue eyes.

The orchestra stops to
tune up on the playground—
h.o.r.s.e. with laughter and
soft jeers at Hope's misfire
just before first bell,
the scatter of children
gathering to lines.

Monday's violin now
screeches little lamb's solo
to Mr. Wagner's gentle encouragement,
another cello's heartstrings
gone quiet in the corner,
left by the boy
who just discovered girls.

Michael E. Strosahl

Aurelio's Voice

shimmers,
a silver kayak
on a river
of bruised
night sky

curls like a taste
of country butter
slowly melting over
a craggy crust

it's the tenor of the sun
crooning blue verbs
in the halls
of the house
of the moon

the cerulean glow
glamouring the star-dark
pitch of a four-a.m. city

a tender turn of skin,
a ransom paid in longing
that refuses to burn out
though a hurricane mouth
hisses in its ear

a waterfall
of used tears
iced blue
in the stark
harsh desert
of morning

it's the secret commerce
of the tongue in the dark,
speaking the way
birds dream,
wishing
they had
hands

Mark Sebastian Jordan

Tongue

The star-barks of matter
chirp your name like
the crickets of August,
a dry, high rattle
that crinkles like ice.
I dream of a winter fire
with you by my side.
Urges are gravity,
and sex is math—
I seek a summer shoulder
for a January night,
someone to sail with me
on the glitter-trash jams
of serpentine dreams,
an altar to throw myself
on the mercy of your smile,
so expressive,
so exhausting,
or is that my byline?
strung out to the stars
with threads of influence,
trembling with the nowness,
of the nothingness that
populates our atoms.

There's nothing there, and that's everything.

So don't tell me there's no magic:
I've licked the physics;
I can tell you its taste.

Mark Sebastian Jordan

Return

In this shell of an ear,
Pacific waves …
light roll, dim crash, gentle pull.

I stroll on whale rock, black, porous.
Side of orange stars, breathing there.

Suspended in pools, a shimmering green
purrs under the wind's touch.

I shelter under pine swept low and blue,
crouch over sanded sneakers.

The ocean sky cracks in simple scarlet streaks.
My sigh sets the sun.

Cynthia Hahn

I'm Dreaming Nightmares

I watch my fingers
moving through the air,
my sharp needle
trying to weave white threads
floating in my brain
into a sensible quilt
because I am cold.
I unload a truck heaped with items
I do not need,
but I cannot seem to
fill a rusty wheelbarrow fast enough.
I string disorganized thoughts
along a shelf of bright stars,
winding through faraway galaxies.
I hear loud clanging,
high-pitched squealing sounds,
roaring thunder that
I throw into a drum.
Musical notes ring out.
I try to put them into stanzas
to create a concert,
but they instead become a cacophony
of clanging metal
and shattering, breaking glass.
Lights finally dim, and,
at last, a gentler sleep comes.

RM Yager

Modal Improvisation on Celtic Harp

Ionian:

A girl was given a compass that can't be lost.
She grows up wrapped in lullabies, content as flannel.
As a woman, she is free to wander the road to joy.

Dorian:

Plainsong chants float from the abbey windows at vesper dusk
as inks dry on the day's vellum in the scriptorium.

Phrygian:

A woman leans into a cold headwind
and wraps her shawl around her baby
as the boat they boarded days ago
sails farther and farther west.

Lydian:

A new dappled fawn takes its first steps,
wet, wobbly, leaving tiny cloven footprints
in the rain-damp forest floor.

Mixolydian:

A woman whose heart has been broken many times,
sorts through her father's things after his death
and finds a box of letters she wrote him from college
and finds photos and letters from many women
who loved him, before and after her mother.

Aeolian:

Every drop of time falls into a salty pool of grief,
as familiar and needed as rain.
The heart belongs to longing.

Locrian:

So, if our hurts keep hurting
and conflicts reoccur,
is living with no resolution
the only path?

Ionian:

And yet every child is born
looking for home
and able to sing.

                                        Liza Hyatt

Entering a Lilac Blossom

From the distance, the foothills
were blue-pink flesh folded over
the lip of the earth,
and when we entered them,
they remained soft and hazy.
We had reached the place
where distance remains distant
even when it is close.

We grew sad
remembering all the feelings
we expected when we grew older,
but didn't—safety, freedom, praise.

Mountain wrens sang, then silenced.
It began to rain,
and the smell of pine needles
and wet moss on stones
bled into the gray sky,
and suddenly we felt
a sad love for this world
which we never expected.

We followed smooth curves
of rose-quartz-streaked earth
and came to the spine
of a prehistoric bird
curled as a spiral
which we could read
and which said,
"What was is no longer,
and what wasn't will be."

"Does that mean," I asked you,
"what isn't here now
will be here someday?"

You didn't answer
and so I stood with you
listening to the slow arrival
and echo of thunder.

Liza Hyatt

Angel from Illinois

(after John Prine 1946 – 2020)

Hello Mother dearest, it's your little traveling man.
I'm being careful—yes, of course, I am.
We have a missing carpenter from off the rig,
so guess who's making up for all his shifts?

He tells her now that he's left socks unwashed
with gaping holes
in all the crannies of the globe and boarded planes
in shorts and working boots
as he had given his good shoes and jeans
to hotel maids
on non-existent wage
for all their sons—his size, his age?

And then an ache so painful, almost rage
consumes her
for the love of his good, kindly ways.

Ear to ground,
she hears him whisper far
across Atlantic seas—*I'm here, my belly's full*
and I have shoes and beer.
An angel here from Illinois has found
that missing carpenter from off the rig.
He showed the cops where drills and ropes
and blood-impervious nails were kept.

Lois Hambleton

matisse's dog

old red belly is napping
sunny-side up,
a splash on the patio:
white and blue
and gray.
snoring,
he lounges
nude in the sunshine,
his legs splayed, four
leaning fence posts,
his eyes jet-black saucers
yet a complicated
yellow

Jeffrey Spahr-Summers

A Straddle Performer

He had no choice but to straddle
two competing obligations.
Psychoanalytic insights failed to provide
any resolution when a hot patootie
landed on his lap,
leaving him a whorl of tangled knots.
She offered a spectacular whirlwind of love.
For a moment, he felt safe enough
to reach for the ecstatic.

Milton P. Ehrlich

Art History's Splashy Smear

Van Gogh's *Self-Portrait with Bandaged Ear*
supports the received story
of the sliced lobe
wrapped in a soiled sock
and gifted to his favorite whore,
the tale of the crazed artist
art historians love to paint.

The revisionist version
restores Gauguin
to his rightful place
in the canon of infamy,
having grazed Vincent's ear
with his foil, a deft feint
to defend himself
from a madman.

Still, museums continue to spin
their cavalier smear,
their insatiable appetite for color
over bare-backed, black and white facts.

Roger Camp

A Peel to Perfection

In a tiny Tuscan town
branded by the summer sun,
an aged man and myself,
castaways in the shade,
sit in a deserted café.
Alternating between sips
of espresso
and a handful of cherries
polished on my sleeve,
I study the old man
in the dappled light.
I watch as he selects from a bowl
an apple whose skin
resembles the roseate cheeks
of Perugino's angels.

Hands steady,
he opens a pen knife.
Beginning at the stem,
he slowly turns the apple
on a plate
as he cuts continuously
until the apple bares itself
corporeal to the core.
When I depart,
I pass the empty table
and a coil so perfect
a snake would envy its plate.

Roger Camp

Blackout poem and art by Heather A. Smith Blaha

Flora, Hovering

Flora, hovering, would say, "A crow flew
from Donegal to pick a white stone." Then,
fingers fluttering, she'd follow her own cue and
snatch some morsel from my plate.
I cried my three-year-old's outrage as she laughed
and stole another crumb of what I valued most.
My tomboy aunt, who never whined that half
of life seemed closed to her,
now haunts the room-and-kitchen of my past,
her raucous energy and sense of fun
still part of me and will be
till the last Scots-Irish memory fades
and it's all one who snatches what from whom.
That crow could steal each morsel of my life
all for her sake.

Arnold Johnston

Corn Dog

Walking into work,
I notice the distinct scent of corn dogs,
and thinking of corn dogs
makes me think of the state fair.
When I was a kid, we'd go every year.
It was a Big Deal—far bigger than it is these days.

The state fair makes me think of the half-ton hog,
fuzzy yellow ducklings sliding into a water tank,
sheep, cows, horses, and chickens
in every breed and color imaginable.
The animals were always my favorite part despite the smells:
I loved the earthiness of it all.

I got to pet brown-eyed cows,
wiry, wooly skittish sheep,
mammoth, muscled horses.
The feel of hide, coat, and feathers,
the sounds of moo, baa, cock-a-doodle-doo—
the sensations of farm life gave me sensory overload.

Then there were buildings full of produce:
monstrous pumpkins, giant cabbages,
the best beets, carrots, and flowers.
Seeing, smelling, touching them
gave me the desire to grow a garden.

Another building and more stuff—
every commercial item a home could need.
We bought a Vita-Mix and used it for years,
making homemade tomato juice and
soup and pineapple milkshakes.

Next came pianos, organs, and keyboards.
I'd sit down and play
little tunes on expensive grand pianos,

feeling the tension in the keys,
finding one with the perfect tone.
Still, I loved my dad's old Acrosonic the best.

Food!
So much food!
Lemon shake-ups, saltwater taffy,
sausage with green peppers and onions,
elephant ears and ... *corn dogs.*
These were the tastes of the fair.

I miss those fairs and
the way it used to be,
my senses stimulated by
the bigness of it all.
But I think what I miss most are another two senses:
the sense of innocence,
the sense of wonder.

Anybody know where I can get a corn dog?

Passage

Apparitions dance in candlelight,
whispering scented words—
lavender calligraphy
of their days gone swiftly by,
vagabond hearts' lamentations
of all that was close but uncaptured.
And as the candle flame surrenders,
they take passage on drifting smoke
until another flame burns.

John R. Hinton

The Connection

I met a traveler at the club last night, the encounter reminding me of an otherworldly creature in the forest assuming human physical characteristics and form to be relatable: bright yellow bandana, tousled blonde hair falling below his shoulders, olive green shirt with a tortoise printed on the front and back. The tortoise is a favorite of the trickster god Hermes, protector of wayfarers.

"I'm from Lexington. I saw these guys play in Louisville." Warm smile, sweet warm breath. The scent of clean sheets fresh from a clothesline in the sun. We chatted while waiting for the music to start. The band finally took the stage, and my new friend responded to the music with eyes closed, arms outstretched, spinning and dipping so low his long hair swept the floor. I wondered how he was not banging his head on the concrete, not crashing into people. It was as if he possessed some sort of echolocation that let him know exactly where his body was in relation to everything and everyone else in the room, even with his eyes closed. He created his own sacred space, and people flowed around him on their way to and from the bar.

I was dancing too, and every time I closed my eyes, I found myself inside his head, experiencing the music through his senses and not my own. It was disorienting, but I submitted to it and settled into his thoughts and emotions. He was utterly uninhibited—untethered—all lightness and grace. A red-tailed hawk swooping from the sky. I followed him through starlight and around the funky bass riffs as he traversed the liminal; transcendent, he led me down tortuous thorny paths, yet even though it was dark, we emerged unscathed. At times we journeyed beside the sea where it relentlessly lapped the dissolving shore, each step melting away into the watery depths as we joyously danced on, surfing upon arpeggios.

Suddenly—dreamlike—we were poised on the edge of a sheer cliff overlooking the ocean far below. In the distance, I heard a cymbal crash in a crescendo of molten colors. I trusted he knew the way to return safely, and, oblivious to fear, I again closed my eyes and leaped with him.

Paula Morgan

Perceptions

Why does hearing the word *dog* always taste like a meatball? And why does the word *crane* taste like the end of an Almond Joy—the sweet, chewy chocolate-covered coconut part without the almond? Simply repeating the word *crane* makes me crave the candy. I have read synesthesia runs in families. My biological mother died. When I'm alone late at night, I swear her ghost is living in the attic, although sometimes I believe it is a squatter who snuck in when the garage door was once left open for hours. I hear noises up there; I hear humming. Cookies disappear from the kitchen faster than I consume them. Milk too. And Almond Joys, which I buy by the bag. I am fascinated by cranes. I watch documentaries about them and delve into legends about how the Druids kept their magical tools in crane-skin bags. I write poems by moonlight about cranes. I always read my poems aloud to hear if they flow well. There was a full moon last night. This morning, I noticed a partially chocolate-encrusted almond beside the attic door.

Paula Morgan

Oakmont

some trees fall for the thrill of it,
shake out their leaves like they're serenading a strip club
and dive into power lines,
oaks corrupt since an acorn,
garden-rooted saplings hiding out in your rose bushes
shade everything but the patio

the winter roots of disgust,
branches snapped off at the edges of society,
waiting for the rotten warmth of summer,
bird-brained ideas that start at dawn,
pecking at the dirt for signs of life

there's nothing plastic about it,
natural as wet soil on a spring day,
ground that clays up around its favorite daylily,
henpecked ideas lost at soul level,
a stately treebound existence at the river's edge

                              Jordan Krais

Vasectomy

I.

For all the sun outside, the persistent
positivity we put on every morning
like a face, the world is burning. Soon
there will be little left at all
even to commemorate as the oceans
boil away and polar bears, balanced
on what remains of our ice caps,
slip with their great and lumbering grace
back into the sea. And the world,
for all its wondrous things remaining,
already has far too many children
without my help.

II.

In the urologist's office, I remove my clothes
and ease onto the low table.
The nurse drapes around my lower half
a giant unfolding paper, preps
the machine that will,
while chattering on its beeping way, quickly cauterize me
like a tiny, burning sun. The doctor
puts the radio on, pulls out needles,
chats me up. She gets to work,
warns me of the pinch and burn to come,
and gives me drugs to make me numb.
In half an hour, I am done.

III.

Home is a tiny sky-blue marble
on which no one asked to be.

Tyler Robert Sheldon

Bedtime Story

We will tell our children
of a virus, powerful, muscular,
a shapeshifter sprinting through crowds,
trailing entire families into their houses
to subsume their very breath, hop-
skotching through homes for the elderly
with chrysanthemum precision,
picking its prey with a particular logic
denied by partygoers at a Miami bar.

In a Texas church, the faithful
shout hallelujahs, raise their hands
to heaven as the reverend assures them
with providential promises and Biblical
quotes, even as the stealth buds blossom
in their lungs, the clots forming
silent amens.

It's all so beautiful, the microscopic
flowers buried up noses, sidling into throats,
strange anemones with stamens multiplying
in tendrils Medusa would have envied,
ready to sting merrymakers on spring break
before vanishing among the hymns and pews.

In those days, grandmothers who survived
could no longer smell their own cooking,
and children wore masks to school,
like rows of little raccoons. And every time
we thought it was finished, it began again,
another round of schoolyard tag.

Now time for bed, no more questions.
You will dream of a garden with blood-soaked
rhododendrons waiting to scoop you up
in their vampire arms.

Donna Pucciani

Stargazing

I can imagine his good eye glowing
with the energy of priestly youth,
a boyish passion for God
propelling him up the mountain
to the monastery of black-robed monks.

Now, at ninety-six, Zio Ernesto
has fallen in his cell, bruising his spine
already curved like David's harp.

He gives thanks for the pain,
welcomes the therapist each week
who kneads his back like a new-formed loaf
ready for rising in the heat of the day.

He sings a little psalm in his ancient heart.
He resurrects himself, ready at any moment
for his ascension into heaven.

He will join the spray of the sea, a strange
friarly figure swaying in the sky over bikini sands
and beach umbrellas, into the arms of the Divine,
leaving behind his bent back, his one filmy eye,
the other shining at the beatific vision
like the North Star finding its proper Pole.

He will float over the abbey roofs tiled in prayer,
above the Calabrian hills whose names
only he remembers.

Donna Pucciani

Melt

Frozen patches of old grass
emerge from the mounded snow,
breathing the sun's hesitant
glow. *We have arrived, at last,*
they whisper. *We know the secret
of survival.*

The warm hands of morning
pat the earth as if it were
a stray dog wandering at dawn,
not pretty but alive.

Lawns turn from grey to pale green,
a verdant elegy to winter, and twigs
bend to edge the old turf with lace
like my grandmother's tatted hems
on muslin pillowcases, or faded rickrack
on the skirts of her aprons.

Shredded acorns, seedpods, and wisps
of leaves mulch the hosta beds
and clog drainpipes gurgling
with the memory of ice.

The Ides of March become
the ancient promises of prairie flowers
which the kindly woman at the arboretum
lists for me on a scrap of paper,
those most likely to persevere in shade.

Tonight I dream of Jacob's Ladder, Wild Ginger,
pink Turtlehead, the purple spikes of Black Cohosh,
the ringing of Virginia Blue Bells, the vows
of Solomon's Seal pushing through the soft
moss, reaching for the light.

Donna Pucciani

God-Speed

The river, in all its raw beauty, turbulent with light,
is a living, breathing entity of immortality
we will never know,
surrounded by dark odors of fermenting green,
decaying wood, animal scat,
and with rotting fish heads floating on the surface.

A poet wrote that a river runs on god-time.
I feel my own age rushing past on god-speed,
in concurrence with the river flow,
not meandering and slow but in a headlong race,
neck and neck with time.

The river only recognizes the future
as it becomes the past, as we
sometimes do, though rarely.
Memories skim over the water,
small swimmers performing the backstroke.

Kimberly A. Bolton

Lott's Wife

"Lott, do you remember this hill?
I brought you up here before you took me to Kyiv.
I showed you my Baba's and Dido's farm,
their house and barn, and the milk cow."

"I remember, Yana, but we must keep moving.
Beyond the hill, the Russians won't see us."

"I can picture the farm—the garden,
apple and pear trees.
Oh, and sunflowers,
wasn't it beautiful, Lott?"

"Yes, Yana, it was beautiful,
But please, we cannot dwell."

"My knees tremble when the shells explode in the town.
Why is God punishing us?
Why is he punishing Baba and Dido?
Why is he punishing the milk cow?
God should punish me, not them.
I was angry at you, remember,
when you took me to Kyiv,
and I was vain in my new dresses
when we returned to visit.
God should punish me, not the poor milk cow."

"Yana, keep moving. At the top
the smoke from the fires will hide us."

"I hear people crying, Lott.
They are praying for help."

"That's the wind and the fires you hear."

"No, Lott, no. It is Baba.

She is calling Dido.
He must be trying to save something
to take with them. Will they get away?"

"Yana, we begged them to come.
We said we'd help them,
And what did they say?"

"They said this was their home.
This is where their parents were buried.
They said the people here were their people."

"Yana, we tried to help them. Now we must help ourselves.
I plead with you. Keep moving, but do not look back."

"I must rest a moment.
My legs are weak, and I can't breathe.
Lott, listen. The church bells are ringing.
They are ringing for help.
I hear singing. It's Father Marko,
the one with the beautiful voice.
He is singing, 'How long, O Lord?
Why must I see ruin?
Why must I look at misery?'"

"Yana, don't you hear the machine guns?
Nothing is moving in the village
except the Russians and the flames."

"Baba and Dido are coming. I know it.
We must wait. I think I see them."

"I told you not to look.
Those are Russian soldiers you see.
The Russians will shell this hill
when they see it is an escape route."

"Lott, all those people are in agony.
I can't move my legs.
My feet are like stones.
Go without me."

"Yana, come. Come now."

"No, I will wait for Baba and Dido.
In my heart, I know they will come."

"Yana, please."

"You go, Lott, and tell others what you saw here.
All those people, all those children,
some will come out.
I can't move without them.
Go."

John D. Groppe

I Seek Another Season

A weaver calls
into the orange horizon.
It's barely morning,
yet the sky already burns
a blaze of Africa time
across my skin,
each slice of heat cutting
sweet scents of Jacaranda on my tongue
and the slow, dull street hum
creeping into my bones
in symphony swells,
this dryness of the earth, this aching thirst
before thundershowers give birth at night.
My memory serves me well.

Carly D

The Gravedigger of Pompeii

It's him, whistling through the dormancy of trees,
his sharp dirge interrupting our darkness.
He bends and peers into the void,
thrumming over our contours,
embedded in volcanic walls
where the solace and the craving are at odds and required.

Try as he might,
there is no quenching the desire
of a million sparks of pain on fire
forged in cindered flesh and bone.
This, our forms full of craving,
still reaching for one another.

Carly D

Russian River Pinot Noir

With its aromas of rose petal
and freshly turned earth,
this dark wine
makes a delicious statement
on the power of blending grapes
from vineyards all over
the Russian River Valley,
revealing tangy layers
of boysenberry, cranberry,
and black tea
against accents of clove,
cardamon, *herbes de Provence*,
and orange peel.

In other words, it is so good
it will pull down your petals,
smooth out your bottom layer,
and kick you in the accents.

David Lee Garrison

Oriole

My afternoon nap turns into a party. At first,
only the cat and a maple branch pressing
against the screen. Somewhere on the branch,

between the leaves of sleep and wake, the oriole
arrives, his song so loud that everyone hears,
even the dead. Mary Oliver strides into the room,

fresh from the feathery fields, notebook at the ready.
Will you remember, she asks, the good birds in my poems,
the owl that reads the Book of Revelation, goldfinches

falling like wheels of fire? O Mistress of Images, we say,
how could we forget? Rachel Carson appears,
eyeing the cat. I warned you, she sighs, of spring

without birds. We bow to her courage.
Rachel and the cat purr as if praying in their sleep.
Finally, here's Emily, attuned, as always,

to ecstasy, to ballads, to bards. She laments
that "hope is a thing with feathers" has become
a cliché. Tell me about it, Mary nods.

We all turn to the oriole, little melodeon.
His song feels like rain, like storms,
like wild, precious spring.

Kathryn Dohrmann

Some Poets

Some poets cannot bear a day of solitude.
Some listen to a scarlet bird
rhapsodize, notes that tumble one
by one into a collecting pool where poets
dive to the underside and surface
over and over with words that undulate,
vibrate, quiver into meaning.

Some poets follow bloody bootprints
to empty shells of grief,
capsized mountains, fiery streams
of lava, whirls of wind that wreck

people and homes and nests,
to possibilities that need a turn
of soil, a night's rest to find
vines holding fast to branches
that sway in the wind from
a quaking mother tree.

Rita Coleman

A Taste of Old Times

I could see it leaking
from the heavy hanging curve
of the wild hive.
Lazy gold dribbles
pooling in the tufts of
clover beneath the forest oak.

I wanted to dip my fingers
into that sweet viscosity,
to feel the yielding press
of full comb,
to taste that pure nectar
goodness and remind myself
of summers helping
my grandmother keep bees,
watching her fearless
hands move with sure strength.
If she were still here,
I know one taste would
uncloud her memories
of us, until her eyes
became as clear as that
amber drip.

I stayed my hand,
both in homage to her
who never took
when she could give,
and as a favor to the bees
who had done
the hard work
of bringing
grandma back to me
under that old oak.

Chris Hasara

Interview with Jan Ball, winner of the Editor's Choice Award for Issue Nine

Jan has had nearly four hundred poems published in various journals internationally and in the U.S., including: *ABZ, Mid-American Review, Nimrod,* and *Parnassus.* Finishing Line Press published her three chapbooks and first full-length poetry collection, *I Wanted to Dance with My Father. Orbis,* England, nominated her for the Pushcart Prize in 2020, and Constellations nominated her for it in 2021.

Jan wrote a dissertation at the University of Rochester: *Age and Natural Order in Second Language Acquisition* (1996) after being a Franciscan nun for seven years, then living in Australia for fourteen years with her Aussie husband and two children. Back in the States, Jan taught ESL in Rochester, New York, and Loyola and DePaul Universities in Chicago. When not writing, traveling, or gardening at their farm, Jan and her husband like to cook for friends.

Does where you live color your poetry?

Where I live doesn't always color my poetry because I draw much content from childhood and the seven years I spent as a Catholic nun, but I do tend to write about the Gulf of Mexico and beaches when we are in Florida half the year as snowbirds. We go to a farm regularly when we are in Chicago. I just wrote a poem about a deceptive brown horned owl there, so I was stimulated to write by what I saw around me. We used to go to France every June, and I have many poems published in *The Mediterranean Review.*

How long have you been writing creatively?

I have been writing creatively since I was about twelve. I was encouraged very much to write by excellent English teacher/nuns at St. Benedict's High School in Chicago, but I didn't start submitting work for publication until I had a teacher in Rochester, New York, who assigned a poem and submitted mine for publication in a local journal, *Hazmat*. I must have been in my fifties then. I wish I could remember Michelle's last name or the institution where the course was held so I could thank them.

What is something surprising about yourself that may not be easily perceived through your writing?

People seem very surprised when they hear that I've been a nun. One of my chapbooks is about the convent. In a recent zoom interview, I was surprised that the content became focused on the convent. I don't advertise that I have a doctorate. It's kind of cozy to have written a dissertation tucked into is interested in talking to me, but I never use the title Dr. before my name. We have also traveled extensively which is handy for conversations, too.

Do you have any advice for writers?

Advice for young writers: write a journal, read a lot of poetry, edit your poems, and don't be frustrated by rejections. Michelle taught me, too, that there's a journal for everything.

David Allen is a retired journalist living in central Indiana. His poems have been published in many journals and anthologies. He is a member and past vice president of the Poetry Society of Indiana. He has four books available from Amazon online at: tinyurl.com/davidallenpoet. Visit his poetry blog at www.davidallen.nu.

Jan Ball's poems appear in journals such as: *Calyx, Parnassus*, and *Phoebe*, internationally, and in the U.S. Jan's three chapbooks: *accompanying spouse, Chapter of Faults* and *Day Job*, were published with Finishing Line Press as well as her first full-length poetry book, *I Wanted to Dance with My Father*. *Orbis*, England, nominated one of her poems for The Pushcart in 2020, and *Constellations* nominated her in 2021. Jan was a nun for seven years then met her Aussie husband and lived with him and their two children for fifteen years in Australia. They lived in Rochester, NY for fifteen years where Jan did a doctorate and wrote a dissertation, Age and Natural Order in Second Language Learning. They now live in Chicago half the year and Sarasota, Florida, the other half.

Lois Baer Barr is a literacy tutor in Chicago. Thrice nominated for a Pushcart, Barr was a finalist for the Rita Dove Poetry Prize. Her chapbook *Biopoesis* won Poetica's first prize, and *Tracks: Poems on the "L"* will be out this summer at Finishing Line Press. She bikes with husband Lew, walks with their Golden Doodle Aggie, and dances flamenco. Her website is www.loisbaerbarr.com

Our featured artist **Heather A. Smith Blaha** is an 8th grade art teacher by day, and by night and weekend she tinkers with art and with words. She loves playing with and poking at things to see what she can make. She lives in Elkhart with her husband and her cat and way too many art supplies. If you want to see more of her art in full color, check out her Instagram @lastnightimade.

Mark Blickley grew up within walking distance of New York's Bronx Zoo. He is a proud member of the Dramatists Guild and PEN American Center. His latest book is the flash fiction collection, *Hunger Pains* (Buttonhook Press).

Kimberly Bolton is a folklore poet who began writing poetry at age 45. She was one of 43 poets worldwide to be published in the Poetry Super Highway *Yom Hashoah* issue for spring 2019. Her poems have been performed on stage including her narrative poem *The Tale of Mercy Periwinkle*. Her poetry has been published on the *Medusa's Kitchen Poetry* website and *Last*

Stanza Poetry Journal. She has written two books of folklore poetry, *Folk* and *Tales from Grindstone Creek.* Her third book, *Trees & Broomsticks, is* due out in autumn 2022. She is currently working on her fourth book, *Down in the Holler.* Kimberly lives in Jefferson City, Missouri near her beloved Missouri River.

Michael H. Brownstein's latest volumes of poetry, *A Slipknot to Somewhere Else* (2018) and *How Do We Create Love* (2019) were both published by Cholla Needles Press. In addition, he has appeared in *Skidrow Penthouse, Last Stanza Poetry Journal, American Letters and Commentary, Xavier Review, Hotel Amerika, Meridian Anthology of Contemporary Poetry, The Pacific Review*, Poetrysuperhighway.com, *Café Review,* and others. He has nine poetry chapbooks including *A Period of Trees* (Snark Press, 2004), *Firestorm: A Rendering of Torah* (Camel Saloon Press, 2012), *The Possibility of Sky and Hell: From My Suicide Book* (White Knuckle Press, 2013) and *The Katy Trail, Mid-Missouri, 100 Degrees Outside and Other Poems* (Kind of Hurricane Press, 2013). He is the editor of *First Poems from Viet Nam* (2011).

Roger Camp lives in Seal Beach, CA where he muses over his orchids, walks the pier, plays blues piano, and spends his afternoons with a charm of hummingbirds under an Angel's Trumpet reading. When he's not at home, he's photographing in the Old World. His work has appeared in *Poetry East, Rust+Moth, Gulf Coast, Southern Poetry Review,* and *Nimrod.*

Dan Carpenter is an Indianapolis journalist, blogger, and writer and lover of poetry. His poems have appeared in many journals and in two collections, *The Art He'd Sell for Love* (Cherry Grove) and *More Than I Could See* (Restoration).

Kathy Jo (KJ) Carter, Urban Dirt Devil, is Indiana to the core, descended from Welsh farmers and Russian/Prussian ethnicity. Retired nurse, musician, and great-grandmother, this mystery buff found a niche in poetry and prose. Who knew? Published in *Indiana Voice Journal, Poets of Madison County, Ink to Paper,* the Poetry Society of Indiana anthology, and *Last Stanza* Journals. Mystery in the works! Kathy is a member of Last Stanza Poetry Society.

Alys Caviness-Gober is a disabled anthropologist, artist, and writer. She taught Anthropology, Women's Studies, and ESOL at the university level, and was a PhD candidate in Applied Linguistics until her disabilities worsened in 2009. In 2011, Alys began selling artwork (*Creative Expressions Arts*), and soon after was juried into the *Hamilton County Artists' Association* in both their photography and 2D categories. Alys and author Sarah E. Morin are the cofounders of the literature-based annual project *Noblesville Interdisciplinary Creativity Expo* (NICE). In November 2014, Alys founded *Logan Street Sanctuary, Inc.* (LSS), an all-volunteer 501(c)(3) Arts organization and the organization took over hosting the annual *Noblesville Interdisciplinary Creativity Expo* (NICE) project and in 2016 took over publishing the annual anthology *The Polk Street Review*. In July 2019, LSS rebranded as *Community • Education • Arts* (CEArts). Alys is a FY2017 (July 2016 - June 2017) Indiana Arts Commission *Individual Artist Project* Grant Award recipient, for which she created a series of large-scale paintings expressing life with hidden disabilities. She was selected to participate in the IUPUI Arts and Humanities Institute's *Religion Spirituality, and the Arts* 2018/19 Seminar Class, and has been an invited presenter at *Poetry Society of Indiana* conferences since 2017. Alys is a selected poet for *INverse: Indiana's Poetry Archive*, and a member of both *Noble Poets* and the *Poetry Society of Indiana*. Alys' poetry has been featured in global anthologies since the 1980s, in the *Last Stanza Poetry Journal*, *The Polk Street Review*, and in her own poetry and artwork collections, *Naked In Wonderland (Volumes I, II, III, IV)*. She serves on the Noblesville Cultural Arts Council and is active in the local arts scene. Alys' artwork, photographs, and poetry have received national and international recognition.

Jan Chronister is the author of five chapbooks and two full-length poetry collections. She lives within sight of Lake Superior.

Rita Coleman resides in rural Greene County, Ohio, with her husband, Frank, their dog, Boo Boo, and their rabbit, Nova. Rita writes award-

winning poetry and has been published in numerous anthologies including *Pine Mountain Sand and Gravel*, *I Thought I Heard a Cardinal Sing*, and *Living and Dying with Covid-19* (UK). Rita has published two poetry chapbooks, *Mystic Connections* and *And Yet*. Her full-length poetry collection, *In the Near Distance*, has been accepted and will be published by Finishing Line Press in 2022. Rita holds a B.A. and an M.A. in English, Creative Writing, Wright State University.

Carly D has published a few poems and short stories in various lit mags and anthologies such as *Ekphrastic Review, Royal Rose, All World's Wayfarer, CP Quarterly,* and *TL;DR Press.* When she is not teaching at a local university, she enjoys working on her poetry and staring off into space. She resides in British Columbia, Canada.

Kathryn Dohrmann has taught for many years in both the Psychology and Environmental Studies Departments at Lake Forest College. Her poems have been published in *CALYX, The Chicago Tribune, The A-3 Review, The Ekphrastic Review, The Last Stanza Poetry Journal, Thema, Nature Folklore, Turning Wheel: The Journal of the Buddhist Peace Fellowship, Collaborative Visions: The Poetic Dialogue Project,* and other publications.

Bruce Ducker's numerous poems and stories have been published in leading journals, including in *The New Republic; the Yale, Southern, Sewanee, Literary, American Literary, Missouri,* and *Hudson Reviews; Shenandoah; Commonweal; the New York Quarterly; the PEN/America Journal;* and *Poetry Magazine.* The prize-winning author of eight novels and a book of short fictions, he lives in Colorado.

Milton P. Ehrlich, Ph.D. is a 90-year-old psychologist and a veteran of the Korean War. He has published many poems in periodicals such as the *London Grip, Arc Poetry Magazine, Descant Literary Magazine, Wisconsin Review, Red Wheelbarrow, Christian Science Monitor,* and *The New York Times.*

The poetry of **David Lee Garrison** has been read by Garrison Keillor on "The Writer's Almanac" and featured by Ted Kooser in his column, "American Life in Poetry." Named Ohio Poet of the Year in 2014, his most recent book is *Light in the River* (Dos Madres Press).

John D. Groppe, Professor Emeritus at Saint Joseph's College, Rensselaer, IN, has published in *Tipton Poetry Journal, Flying Island, From the Edge of the Prairie, Christianity Today, The National Catholic Reporter,* and other journals. His poem "A Prophet Came to Town" was nominated for a Pushcart Prize (2013). His poem "Sudden Death" won honorable mention in Embers poetry contest (1984). His poetry collection *The Raid of the Grackles and Other Poems* (Iroquois River Press) was published in 2016. He is listed on the Indiana Bicentennial Literary Map 200 Years: 200 Writers.

Cynthia T. Hahn has two published books of poetry, *Outside-In-Sideout* (Finishing Line Press, 2011) and *Coïncidences* (alfAbarre, 2014), the first

on the process of grieving, and the second a bilingual (French-English) poetic journey of a women's life. Hahn is Professor of French at Lake Forest College, IL, and teaches creative writing, translation, and Francophone literatures. She has translated over a dozen novels by Lebanese, Algerian and French writers. She plays bass ukulele and West African drums; poetry is found in the rhythms.

Born in Birmingham UK, **Lois Hambleton** has poetry published by *Culture Matters Co-Operative Ltd, Poetry Bus, The Madrigal Press, Transcendent Zero Press, Anti-Heroin Chic, Last Stanza Poetry Journal,* and others. Her professional life has been spent teaching in adult education and rehabilitation units. She writes about alcoholism with work included in two addiction anthologies: *A Wild and Precious Life* (Unbound) and *Despite Knowing* (Fore Street Press).

Chris Hasara is a father of four and husband of one in Northern Indiana. He studied creative writing at Western Kentucky University and has applied that education to a successful career as a truck driver and farmer. His words have appeared in *From the Edge of the Prairie,* recent volumes of *The Last Stanza Poetry Journal,* and volume 6 of the Poetry Society of Indiana book *Ink to Paper.*

John R. Hinton is an Indiana poet and writer. His writing is inspired by our

daily human interactions and the accompanying emotions: love, hate, indifference, passion. His words explore who we are, how we behave. Sometimes eloquent, other times gritty, these words seek to reveal the joy and pain of living this beautiful human existence. He is the author of two poetry collections: *Blackbird Songs* and *Held.* John is the President of the Poetry Society of Indiana and a member of Last Stanza Poetry Association.

Liza Hyatt is an art therapist from Indianapolis. Her publications include three books of poetry and two chapbooks, including: *Under My Skin* (Wordtech Editions, 2012); *Stories Made of World,* (Finishing Line Press, 2013), *The Mother Poems* (Chatter House Press, 2014); *Once, There Was a Canal* (Chatter House Press, 2017). She is also the author of a

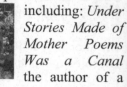

book of art practices to enhance Earth-stewardship: *Art of the Earth: Ancient*

David James' most recent book is *Alive in Your Skin While You Still Own It*, Kelsay Books, 2022. He teaches at Oakland Community College.

Arnold Johnston's latest poetry collection is *The Infernal Now*, just out from Kelsay Books. His poetry, fiction, non-

fiction, and translations have appeared widely in literary journals and anthologies. His plays, and others written in collaboration with his wife, Deborah Ann Percy, have won over 300 productions and readings, as well as numerous awards and publications across the country and internationally; and they've written, co-written, edited, or translated over twenty books. His many accurate English versions of Jacques Brel's songs have appeared in musical revues nationwide, and are also featured on his CD, *Jacques Brel: I'm Here!* A performer-singer, Arnie has played many solo concerts and over 100 roles on stage, screen, and radio. He is a member of the Dramatists Guild, Poets & Writers, the Associated Writing Programs, and the American Literary Translators Association. He was chairman of the English Department (1997-2007) and taught for many years at Western Michigan University, where he co-founded the creative writing program and founded the playwriting program. He is now a full-time writer. Johnston-Percy-Writers.com

Mark Sebastian Jordan has written, produced, directed, and acted in numerous theater pieces. He is the author of History Knox, a weekly local history column on KnoxPages.com. He has written program notes for the Cleveland Orchestra, the Mansfield Symphony, and other musical ensembles, as well as delivering many music appreciation talks. He is the author of *The Ceely Rose Murders at Malabar Farm* (The History Press), *The Book of Jobs* (Pudding House Press), *Murder Ballads* (Poets' Haven Press), and *1776 & All That* (XOXOX Press), and has received an excellence award from the Ohio Arts Council for his musical criticism. He has been seen on TV in *Ghost Hunters*, *Mysteries at the Museum*, and *My Ghost Story*. He appeared as a background actor in *The Shawshank Redemption* and has given many talks and tours about that experience.

Jenny Kalahar is the editor and publisher of *Last Stanza Poetry Journal.* She is the founding leader of Last Stanza Poetry Association in Elwood, Indiana. Jenny and her husband, poet Patrick, are used and rare booksellers. She was the humor columnist for *Tails Magazine* for several years and the treasurer for Poetry Society of Indiana. Author of fifteen books, she was twice nominated for a Pushcart Prize and once for Best of the Net. Her poems have been published in journals, anthologies, and newspapers. Her works can be found on poemhunter.com and *INVerse,* Indiana's poetry archive. Through Stackfreed Press, she has published books for numerous authors. Contact her at laststanza@outlook.com

Patrick Kalahar is a used and rare bookseller with his wife, Jenny, and a book conservationist. He is a veteran, world traveler, avid reader, and book collector. He is a member of Last Stanza Poetry Association. His poems have been published in *Tipton Poetry Journal, Flying Island, Rail Lines, The Moon and Humans, Polk Street Review, Northwest Indiana Literary Journal,* and *A Disconsolate Planet.* Patrick can be seen as an interviewee in the Emmy-winning documentary *James Whitcomb Riley: Hoosier Poet,* and he gives costumed and scholarly readings as Edgar Allan Poe.

Jordan Krais is a poet from the north shore of Long Island. He's spent most of the last two years roaming the river near his home. You can find him on Instagram @captain_hawthorne where he posts pictures of the river and the stuff he types on his typewriter.

Norbert Krapf, former Indiana Poet Laureate, will have released in the fall his fifteenth poetry collection, *Spirit Sister Dance,* and next spring, his third prose memoir, *Homecomings: A Writer's Memoir,* which covers the fifty plus years of his writing and publishing life. Norbert is looking forward to spending most of the month of August with his Colombian-German-American grandson Peyton, who will turn eight on the 17th of that month in Indy with his grandparents and his Colombian mother helping to celebrate the occasion. Author photo is by Andreas Riedel.

Martin Marcus has written for radio and TV and is a published novelist and humorist with two books of ethnic humor, one a national bestseller. His essays, memoirs, short fiction, and verse have appeared in national and regional magazines, and his poetry has been published in literary journals. Of his collection, *File Under Melancholy,* Pulitzer Prize poet Maxine

Kumin wrote: "Lucky for us that Martin Marcus has returned to his first love, poetry. There's not a false note in this bravura performance."

Mona Mehas writes about growing up poor, accumulating grief, and climate change. As a disabled retired teacher in Indiana, she spends most days at her laptop with two old cats as chaperones. In the past, Mona used the pseudonym, Patience Young. She's been published in *Moments Between*, *The Polk Street Review 2022*, *Loft Books Issue III*, and others. During the early pandemic she watched every Star Trek show and movie in chronological order and many online concerts. Follow on Twitter @Patienc7773209? or see all her publications at linktr.ee/monaiv.

During a career practicing and teaching at UCLA's Department of Psychiatry, **William H. Miller** published three books: *Personal Stress Management for Medical Patients*, *Systematic Parent Training*, and a memoir, *Soothing: Lives of a Child Psychologist*. poems are currently forthcoming in the anthologies *HOPE 2022* (Moonstone Arts Center, 2022) and *Nonsense Verse* (Moonstone Arts Center, 2022).

Paula Morgan lives in Noblesville, Indiana. Her writing is inspired by music, travels, nature, and all things liminal. In the past, she wrote a quarterly column entitled "Embracing Other Realms" for the online magazine, *Faezine*. Their tagline was "Living in the Magic." It is a belief she wholeheartedly endorses.

Samuel Prestridge lives in Athens, Georgia. He has been published in *Literary Imagination*, *Style*, *The Arkansas Review*, *As It Ought To Be*, *Poetry Quarterly*, *Appalachian Quarterly*, *Paideuma*, *The Lullwater Review*, *Poem*, and *The Southern Humanities Review*. "I write poetry," he says, "because there are matters that cannot be directly stated, but that are essential to the survival of whatever soul we can still have. Also, I'm no good at interpretive dance, which is the only other option that's occurred to me." He is a post-aspirational man whose first book, *A Pebble's Worth of Riot, A Dog's Job of Work*, seeks publication.

Donna Pucciani, a Chicago-based writer, has published poetry worldwide in *Poetry Salzburg, ParisLitUp, Meniscus, Shi Chao Poetry, Journal of Italian Translation, Agenda, Stand,* and others. Her work has been translated into Italian, Chinese, Japanese, and German. She has been nominated numerous times for the Pushcart Prize, and has won awards from the Illinois Arts Council, the National Federation of State Poetry Societies, Poetry on the Lake, and other organizations. Her seventh and most recent book of poems is *Edges*.

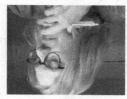

Mary Ellen Reynolds has enjoyed poetry since childhood when her mother raised money for *Poetry Magazine*. She can quote poems, some in French, from long ago. She studied poetry at Northwestern university senior program and at Newberry Library Seminars. A docent at the Lincoln Park Conservatory, she continues to teach in Chicago. Though she has written many poems, this is the first one published.

Royal Rhodes taught classes in global religions, literature, and death & dying for 40 years at Kenyon College. His poems have appeared in various journals, such as *The Montreal Review, The Lyric, Taj Mahal Review, Cholla Needles, Ariel Chart,* and others. He collaborated on poetry/art books with The Catbird [on the Yadkin] Press in North Carolina, and more recently with *Red Wolf Journal*. He has also translated ancient Greek and Latin lyric poetry.

For over 25 years, Mimi Rosenbush worked in film and television production in Chicago, including in film editing, documentary filmmaking, co-directing the Midwest Region for Steven Spielberg's Shoah Foundation, and working at Harpo on Oprah's Book Club team. Mimi then made a career pivot and taught grammar and English Composition at the University of Illinois at Chicago for ten years. In retirement, Mimi has focused on writing creative non-fiction and, more recently, poetry. Her writing work, as well as her photography, can be viewed on her website: https://mimirosenbush.com.

David M. Rubin lives in New Hope, PA and has a Ph.D. in molecular biology. He has led the building of natural language processing systems to order the scientific literature, lectured on protein folding & protein degradation, real world evidence, and Buddhism in ancient India. He has published many scientific articles and short stories, and recently had drawings and poems published in *Ffraid*, short stories in *After Dinner Conversations, Brilliant Flash Fiction* and *The Nabokovian,* and an essay in *The Smart Set.*

Tyler Robert Sheldon's six poetry collections include *When to Ask for Rain* (Spartan Press, 2021), a finalist for the Birdy Poetry Prize. He is Editor-in-Chief of *MockingHeart Review* and his work has appeared in *The Los Angeles Review*, *Pleiades*, *The Tulane Review*, *Tinderbox Poetry Journal*, *The Dead Mule School of Southern Literature*, and other places. A Pushcart Prize nominee and winner of the Charles E. Walton Essay Award, Sheldon earned his MFA at McNeese State University. He lives in Baton Rouge with his spouse, the artist and upholsterer Alexandria Arcenaux.

Jeffrey Spahr-Summers is a poet, writer, photographer, and publisher. His work can be found at www.jeffreyspahrsummers.com

Eric Fisher Stone is a poet and writing tutor from Fort Worth, Texas. He received his MFA in writing and the environment from Iowa State University. His poetry publications include two full length collections: *The Providence of Grass*, from Chatter House Press in 2018, and *Animal Joy*, from WordTech Editions in 2021.

Michael E. Strosahl grew up blocks from the Mississippi, pulled his roots and moved to Indiana, where he discovered the Indianapolis poetry scene, participating in many groups around the state, including Last Stanza. In addition to regularly submitting to this journal, his work appears often in the *Tipton Poetry Journal* and in a weekly blogspot post he does for the site Moristotle & Company. He currently resides between two rivers in Jefferson City, Missouri.

Kelly Talbot has edited books and other content for twenty years for Wiley, Macmillan, Oxford, Pearson Education, and other publishers. His writing has appeared in dozens of magazines and anthologies. He divides his time between Indianapolis, Indiana and Timisoara, Romania.

David Vancil's book of poetry, *Expiation: War and Its Aftermath* is forthcoming in early 2023. It deals with his family heritage in warfare and military service from WWI through Vietnam. He's also completed another book tentatively titled *Chameleon in the Kitchen*, which he hopes will also come out in 2023. He resides in Terre Haute.

RM Yager is a retired nurse/teacher/photographer whose topics are marginalized, at risk populations. Poetry is her vehicle to deliver words most people find unspeakable. She hopes to offer inclusion and wants to stop you in your tracks with controversial humor/tragedy within family and relationships, but she also loves whimsy, humor, and nature. She has been published in the US and internationally.

Judy Young is a lifelong Elwood, Indiana poet and member of Last Stanza Poetry Association, the Poetry Society of Indiana, and the National Federation of State Poetry Societies. She is married with five children, nine grandbabies, and seven great-grandchildren. She is the author of *Wild Wood* and *Moonset*, and has been published in *Tipton Poetry Journal*, *Indiana Voice Journal*, and in several anthologies and other journals. She is a nature advocate and tree enthusiast.